Thanks

Written & Illustrated by
Suzi Linden

Thanks for the sunrise
and the call of the birds

thanks for the chickens
and the morning eggs

Thanks for hot coals to start the fire

thanks for the hope
of the first tulip

Thanks
for blue
sky

Thanks
for the
softening
of the
ground

thanks for creeks
to hope

Thanks
for tiny tree blossoms

thanks
for snacks
CREAM
CHEESE

thanks for tomato sandwiches
MAYO

Hthanks for corn on the
cob

thanks for perrenials

thanks
for horses

thanks for pebbles and feathers

thanks for big lakes

thanks
for floats
and docks

thanks
for picnics

thanks for dragonflies

Thanks for wells

thanks for public spaces

thanks for gardens and hobbies

thanks for hot tubs and clotheslines

thanks for the ocean

thanks for campfires

thanks for home

Thanks For Your Time.
Thanks For Your Attention.

In Gratitude
Suzi Linden

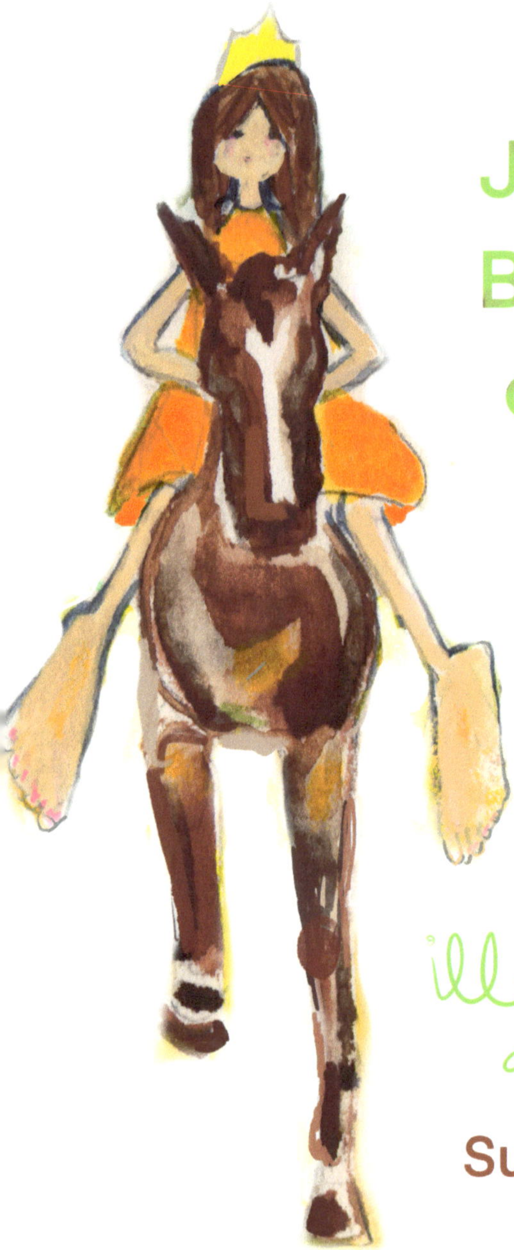

Join Princess Bigfoot in her other books

Princes Bigfoot in Alaska

and

On the Way

illustrations available

SuziLinden.com

LINDEN PRESS PUBLISHING

LINDENPRESSPUBLISHING@GMAIL.COM

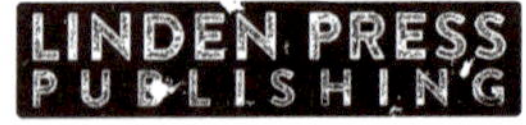

www.ingramcontent.com/pod-product-compliance
Lightning Source LLC
Chambersburg PA
CBHW040949110726
48006CB00007B/1324